CIVILIZATIONS OF THE ANCIENT WORLD

ANCIENT EGYPT

A MyReportLinks.com Book

NEIL D. BRAMWELL

MyReportLinks.com Books
an imprint of

 Enslow Publishers, Inc. **E**
Box 398, 40 Industrial Road
Berkeley Heights, NJ 07922
USA

MyReportLinks.com Books, an imprint of Enslow Publishers, Inc. MyReportLinks® is a registered trademark of Enslow Publishers, Inc.

Library of Congress Cataloging-in-Publication Data

Bramwell, Neil D., 1932–
  Ancient Egypt / Neil D. Bramwell.
    v. cm. — (Civilizations of the ancient world)
  Includes bibliographical references and index.
  Contents: Hatshepsut, king of Egypt—Land, people, and religion—
Arts and cultural contributions — Family Life and education—
Government—History and conquest.
  ISBN 0-7660-5252-4
  1. Egypt—Civilization—To 332 B.C.—Juvenile literature. [1.
Egypt—Civilization—To 332 B.C.] I. Title. II. Series.
  DT61.B6783 2004
  932—dc22

                           2003023615

Printed in the United States of America

10 9 8 7 6 5 4 3 2 1

To Our Readers:
Through the purchase of this book, you and your library gain access to the Report Links that specifically back up this book.
The Publisher will provide access to the Report Links that back up this book and will keep these Report Links up to date on **www.myreportlinks.com** for three years from the book's first publication date.
We have done our best to make sure all Internet addresses in this book were active and appropriate when we went to press. However, the author and the Publisher have no control over, and assume no liability for, the material available on those Internet sites or on other Web sites they may link to.
The usage of the MyReportLinks.com Books Web site is subject to the terms and conditions stated on the Usage Policy Statement on **www.myreportlinks.com**.
A password may be required to access the Report Links that back up this book. The password is found on the bottom of page 4 of this book.
Any comments or suggestions can be sent by e-mail to comments@myreportlinks.com or to the address on the back cover.

Photo Credits: © Corel Corporation, pp. 1, 3, 11, 25, 26, 30, 31, 34, 37, 38; Ancient Scripts.com, p. 28; Art Images for College Teaching, p. 21; BBC, p. 19; Emory University, p. 40; Enslow Publishers, Inc., p. 14; Giza On Line, p. 17; PBS, p. 42; MyReportLinks.com Books, pp. 4, back cover; Photos.com, p. 15.

Cover Photos: King Tutankhamen, Khufu pyramid, and Nefertiti, © Corel Corporation.

Contents

ANCIENT
EGYPT

MyReportLinks.com Books
Great Books, Great Links, Great for Research!

The Report Links listed on the following four pages can save you hours of research time by **instantly** bringing you to the best Web sites relating to your report topic.

How to Use MyReportLinks.com

1 Got a Report to do?

2 Check out a MyReportLinks.com Book at the Library.

3 Read the Book.

4 Go to www.myreportlinks.com for Quick, Safe, and Up-to-Date Links!

5 Internet Report Links = Great Information.

6 Write Your Report. Impress Your Teacher.

MAX LYNX

The pre-evaluated Web sites are your links to source documents, photographs, illustrations, and maps. They also provide links to dozens—even hundreds—of Web sites about your report subject.

MyReportLinks.com Books and the MyReportLinks.com Web site save you time and make report writing easier than ever!

Please see "To Our Readers" on the copyright page for important information about this book, the MyReportLinks.com Web site, and the Report Links that back up this book. Please enter **VEG3720** if asked for a password.

▶Egyptians
*EDITOR'S CHOICE

This BBC Interactive Web site provides an in-depth exploration of ancient
Egypt. It includes articles on hieroglyphs, ancient Egyptian magic, Hatshepsut,
and more.

▶Pyramids: The Inside Story
*EDITOR'S CHOICE

Learn about the Sphinx, Menkaure's Pyramid, Khafre's Pyramid,
and Khufu's Pyramid at this PBS Web site. You can also take a virtual tour
of the Great Pyramid.

▶The British Museum: Ancient Egypt
*EDITOR'S CHOICE

This British Museum Web site explores many aspects of Egyptian life,
including gods and goddesses, mummification, pharaohs, pyramids, temples,
and writing.

▶The Ancient Egyptian Culture Exhibit
*EDITOR'S CHOICE

At the Ancient Egyptian Culture Exhibit Web site you can learn about everyday
living in ancient Egypt, art, hieroglyphs, religion, government, and much more.

▶Mummies of Ancient Egypt
*EDITOR'S CHOICE

This Smithsonian Institution site examines mummies of ancient Egypt.
Learn what mummies are, how they are made, who they were, and why they
were preserved.

▶Nova: Explore Mysteries of the Nile
*EDITOR'S CHOICE

This PBS Web site features images of ancient Egyptian architecture, including
the Luxor Temple and the Colossus of Memnon.

Report Links

▶**Ancient Art and Architecture**

Explore the architecture of ancient Egypt at the Ancient Art and Architecture Web site.

▶**Ancient Egypt Discovery Case**

This Web site provides time lines, interactive maps, and information about religion and burial customs in ancient Egypt.

▶**Ancient Egyptian Scripts**

At the Ancient Egyptian Scripts Web site you can explore the origins and features of hieroglyphs.

▶**At the Tomb of Tutankhamen**

Explore the historic 1923 opening of King Tutankhamen's tomb at this *National Geographic* Web site. Here you will learn about the opening of the tomb and its contents.

▶**BBC: *Egypt's Golden Empire***

Explore Egypt's history, including information about Hatshepsut and Akhenaten, at this Web site.

▶**Cleopatra**

At the Cleopatra Web site you will find a time line of ancient Egyptian art, a glossary of definitions, and maps.

▶***Cleopatra and Egypt***

This PBS Web site explores Cleopatra's role in Egyptian history and tells the story of her relationship with Marc Antony.

▶**Egypt**

Learn about the people, mythology, daily life, writings, and death and burial customs of ancient Egypt in this site.

Report Links

The Internet sites described below can be accessed at http://www.myreportlinks.com

▶**Egypt**

This site from the Detroit Institute of Arts focuses on ancient Egyptian art. It also examines the ancient Egyptian belief in an afterlife.

▶**Egypt—A Country Study**

The Library of Congress provides a comprehensive history of Egypt, including the history of ancient, medieval, and modern Egypt.

▶*Egypt's Golden Empire*

Egypt's Golden Empire, a PBS Web site, provides time lines and interactive maps of ancient Egypt. It also examines what it was like to live in ancient Egypt.

▶**Egyptian Hieroglyphs**

At the Egyptian Hieroglyphs Web site you can learn about the complex writing system known as hieroglyphics.

▶**Egyptian Mummies**

Read about the process of mummification. Discover who was mummified, and learn how scientists study mummies today.

▶**The Egyptian Pyramid**

This Smithsonian Institution Web site offers a brief but informative description of the pyramids of Egypt.

▶**Giza On Line**

At the Giza On Line Web site you can learn about the Sphinx and stone technology. Links to relevant Web sites are included.

▶**Life in Ancient Egypt**

The Carnegie Museum of Natural History explores life in ancient Egypt. Here you will find a chronology of ancient Egyptian dynasties as well as information about daily life, the afterlife, and gods and religion.

Report Links

**The Internet sites described below can be accessed at
http://www.myreportlinks.com**

▶**Mummies Unmasked**

At this *National Geographic* Web site you will learn about the ancient Egyptians' belief in life after death and their preparations for it.

▶**Mysteries of Egypt**

Explore Egyptian archaeology, art, civilization, culture, and many other interesting topics at the Mysteries of Egypt Web site.

▶**Nova: "Pharaoh's Obelisk"**

On this PBS Web site you can explore how obelisks were created as well as how big these structures were, how Egyptians transported them, and how they were erected.

▶**Permanent Collection: Ancient Egyptian Art**

Explore Emory University's permanent collection of ancient Egyptian art.

▶**The Quest for Immortality: Treasures of Ancient Egypt**

The Quest for Immortality Web site provides a virtual tour of Thutmose III's tomb, a slide show, and more from ancient Egypt.

▶*Secrets of the Pharaohs*

Secrets of the Pharaohs, a PBS Web site, provides a time line, historical maps, and other interesting information on the kings of ancient Egypt.

▶**Theban Mapping Project**

The Theban Mapping Project provides tours of the Valley of the Kings and the Theban Necropolis.

▶**Three Cities**

On this site from *National Geographic*, you can see how life has changed over the years. Compare life in Alexandria, Egypt, in A.D. 1 to life in Córdoba, Spain, in A.D. 1000 and New York City in A.D. 2000.

Time Line

?–3100 B.C.	Earliest known communities in ancient Egypt established	
c.3100–2682 B.C.	*Early Dynastic / Archaic*	Upper and Lower Egypt are united. First Egyptian dynasty—rule by members of the same family—established by King Menes.
c.2686–2181 B.C.	*Old Kingdom*	Construction of the pyramids begins.
c.2180–2040 B.C.	*First Intermediate Period*	Political chaos is the norm.
c.2040–1730 B.C.	*Middle Kingdom*	Stability recovered.
c.1730–1550 B.C.	*Second Intermediate Period*	Invasion of Hyksos.
c.1550–1080 B.C.	*New Kingdom*	Egyptian Empire created, and Akhenaton's religious strategy is begun. Reigns of Thutmose I, II, III, and IV; Hatshepsut; Tutankhamen; and Nefertiti.
c.1080–664 B.C.	*Third Intermediate Period*	Divided rule by Libyans, Nubians, and Assyrians in succession.
c.664–332 B.C.	*Late Period*	The Late Period is divided by some into the Saite Period (664–525 B.C.), when a king from the city of Sais in the Delta ruled a unified Egypt, and the Late Period (525–332 B.C.), when the Persian Empire ruled Egypt. Greek rule began with Alexander the Great, in 332 B.C.

Chapter 1

HATSHEPSUT– KING OF EGYPT

On a temple wall at Thebes, Hatshepsut, king of Egypt, commissioned a scene depicting her birth as a divine child. It was Hatshepsut's way to establish her claim to rule as king. Hatshepsut was a woman and could have ruled Egypt as its queen. There were ruling queens of Egypt before and after Hatshepsut, but queens could not exercise all the powers of a king, particularly those of High Priest of Egypt, and Hatshepsut was determined to rule with *all* the powers of the king.

▶ Hatshepsut's Regency

Thutmose III became pharaoh, or king, of Egypt around 1479 B.C., on the death of Thutmose II, his father and Hatshepsut's husband. Thutmose III, Hatshepsut's stepson, was a child at the time, so Hatshepsut was made regent—one who governs until a child becomes old enough to rule.

But Hatshepsut was not content with the limited power that regents had, and by the seventh year of the regency (1473 B.C.), she had become powerful enough to declare herself king of Egypt.[1]

A female king was extremely rare in Egyptian history. Of the hundreds of kings, only four are known to have been women.[2] Hatshepsut ruled with all the power of a male king. To fortify her image as king, Hatshepsut wore the official dress of a male pharaoh when performing official functions, and the images of her found on the temples and monuments show this. For Hatshepsut, the official male dress, which consisted of a short kilt, the male head-dress, and at times, even a false beard, symbolized the male king's absolute power. Hatshepsut was not pretending to be a man, though. Statues and other images of her show her with the body of a female.[3]

▶ Coruler

Hatshepsut did not remove Thutmose III from the throne. Officially, she ruled as co-king, but Hatshepsut exercised sole power for about twenty years. During her rule, Egypt was for the most part at peace, except for at least one military campaign in Nubia (modern-day

▲ Hatshepsut's Temple in Deir el-Bahri is one of many structures erected by this pharaoh. Believed to have taken fifteen years to complete, the temple seems to be an extension of the surrounding landscape, indicating harmony between humans and nature.

Sudan), on Egypt's southern border, at which Hatshepsut may have been present.[4] She also sent an expedition to Punt, a land believed to have been located near the Eritrean coast on the Red Sea. The expedition returned with such wonderful products that Hatshepsut had the event recorded on one of the walls in her temple at Deir el-Bahri.[5]

▶ Deir el-Bahri

Throughout her reign, Hatshepsut built and restored numerous temples and monuments. One of the world's most beautiful buildings commissioned by Hatshepsut is Deir el-Bahri. Chapels for Hatshepsut and her father, Thutmose I, were built as part of this temple. It was here that she had inscribed a scene showing her father declaring Hatshepsut his successor as king.[6] She used this fantasy as propaganda to support her position.

About the twentieth year of her reign as king, Hatshepsut disappears from the Egyptian record. Nothing is known of her death. Thutmose III asserted his right to rule and did so for another thirty-two years as one of Egypt's most powerful kings and military leaders.[7]

In the last years of Thutmose III's rule, a deliberate campaign was conducted throughout Egypt to destroy all statues and pictures of Hatshepsut in an attempt to erase memory of her reign. Historians at first believed hatred of Hatshepsut's rule was the cause of the destruction. Now, politics, not hatred, is thought to have been the motive.

Thousands of years later, the discoveries of the magnificent temple of Deir el-Bahri and the tomb Hatshepsut commissioned to be built in the Valley of the Kings have once again brought King Hatshepsut to life.

LAND, PEOPLE, AND RELIGION

Through the years, the lands of ancient Egypt varied in size and name. The region of southern Egypt from the First Cataract, or waterfall, to Memphis, the first capital of unified Egypt, is called Upper Egypt. The region from Memphis to the Mediterranean Sea, which includes the area known as the "Delta," a broad triangular region, is called Lower Egypt. When unified, Upper and Lower Egypt were known as the "Two Lands."[1]

▶ Ancient Egypt: A Time Line

Ancient Egypt's oldest civilization, thousands of years before Upper and Lower Egypt were united in 3100 B.C., is known as the Predynastic Period. Scholars often disagree on the exact dates for events in ancient Egypt. For example, some historians date the unification of Upper Egypt and Lower Egypt into one kingdom at 2850 B.C.[2]

Historians divide the history of ancient Egypt into three periods beginning with its unification: the Old Kingdom (2686–2181 B.C.), the Middle Kingdom (2040–1730 B.C.), and the New Kingdom (1550–1080 B.C.). These kingdoms were periods in which the absolute rule of kings established a powerful central government. Periods between the kingdoms, when central government was weak, were known as Intermediate Periods, and there were three: the First Intermediate Period (2180–2040 B.C.), the Second Intermediate Period (1730–1550 B.C.), and the Third Intermediate Period (1080–664 B.C.).

A map of ancient Egypt during the New Kingdom (1550 B.C.–1080 B.C.)

Finally, there is the Late Period (664–332 B.C.). It is divided by some into the Saite Period (664–525 B.C.), when a king from the city of Sais in the Delta ruled a unified Egypt, and the Late Period (525–332 B.C.), when the Persian Empire ruled Egypt.[3] Rule by the Greeks, under Alexander the Great, began in 332 B.C.

▶ Nile River: Source of Greatness

The Nile River was key to the development of Egypt as a nation and to its ancient civilization. The Nile runs the entire length of Egypt from the First Cataract at the southern border of ancient Egypt, north to the Delta, where it divides into branches and finally empties into the Mediterranean Sea. The Nile was the only water source the Egyptians had. Each year during the fall, flooding of the Nile deposited a strip of immensely fertile soil about four to thirteen miles wide on both sides of the river.[4]

Deserts and Oases

To the east and west of the fertile land close to the Nile were vast deserts. The deserts of Egypt were not barren wastes, however, but were rich sources of gold and different types of stone, such as granite, limestone, basalt, and alabaster. Vast amounts of stone were quarried from the deserts and mountains for the enormous building projects of the Egyptian kings.

In the desert to the west of Egypt were small isolated pockets of fertile land known as oases. These were linked by trade routes to Libya in the west and to Nubia along Egypt's southern border.[5]

▲ *The Nile, the world's longest river, was ancient Egypt's lifeline, providing a desert land with its only source of water.*

▶ Irrigation and Agriculture

Flooding of the Nile River was so efficient, not only at supplying rich soil but also in washing out the salts deposited over time, that little irrigation was required except for reclamation of the land, or restoring its usefulness. Irrigation consisted of building channels to divert the floodwaters, and dikes and riverbanks had to be maintained to contain them.

A shaduf was the main device used for irrigation by ancient Egyptians. It was simply a long pole mounted on a pivot. The pole had a weight on one end, and a bucket at the other. The bucket was dipped into the water, and the filled bucket was lifted and the water dumped onto the field.[6]

Farmers used wooden plows to produce crops of barley, wheat, vegetables, and flax, which was woven into linen by women.[7] Beer, made from barley, was an important part of the Egyptian diet. The swampy marshes provided safety and food for large numbers of waterfowl, such as ducks and geese, and provided an abundant source of papyrus reeds.

Papyrus had many uses in ancient Egypt. It was twisted into rope and woven to make baskets, mats for roofs, and window coverings. Papyrus was even used in making boats. However, its most important use was in the making of paper.[8]

▶ Ancient Egypt's People

Early in their history, the Egyptians considered themselves one nationality sharing the same beliefs and culture, but they also recognized that they were made up of different groups. From the period of the New Kingdom, the tomb

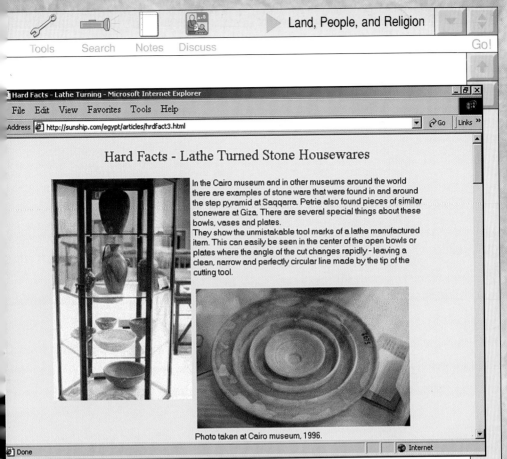

Hard Facts - Lathe Turned Stone Housewares

In the Cairo museum and in other museums around the world there are examples of stone ware that were found in and around the step pyramid at Saqqarra. Petrie also found pieces of similar stoneware at Giza. There are several special things about these bowls, vases and plates.

They show the unmistakable tool marks of a lathe manufactured item. This can easily be seen in the center of the open bowls or plates where the angle of the cut changes rapidly - leaving a clean, narrow and perfectly circular line made by the tip of the cutting tool.

Photo taken at Cairo museum, 1996.

Done   Internet

▲ Ancient Egyptians sculpted stone into beautiful housewares such as bowls, vases, and dishes, using techniques that have not been replicated since that time.

of the king known as Seti I contains a picture showing four ethnic groups who made up the Egyptian population: the remtu or native Egyptians, Asiatics or Amu who lived to the east, Nehesiu who lived to the south, and lastly the Timihu who lived to the west. All had different physical characteristics and wore distinctive dress and headgear.[9]

Farmers and Craftsmen

The majority of the people in ancient Egypt were farmers of small plots, but there were also large numbers of skilled

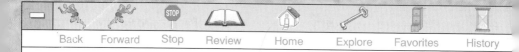
craftsmen employed by the king. Areas of specialization included weaving, medicine, weapon making, food preservation, construction, boat building, brick making, pottery, and working with gold.[10]

Priests

The priesthood formed a large group in ancient Egypt. During certain periods, both men and women served as priests, but most priests were men.[11] As noted earlier, King Hatshepsut assumed the role of high priest during her reign. Most of the priests worked part-time—one month a year. The priests were usually married, and, after serving in the temple, they returned to their families and occupations. Full-time priests wore special costumes.[12]

Religion in Ancient Egypt

Egyptian belief held that in each human there existed the Ka, the spiritual being of that human. The Ka continued its existence after death but required the preservation of its human body and daily offerings of food and drink.[13]

The Egyptians had an enormous number of gods.[14] Every city and village in Egypt had its own special god to whom offerings were made. In ancient Egyptian homes, images of the gods were placed on a small altar where daily prayers were offered.

Custom and the king's beliefs determined the formal worship and rituals of Egyptian religion. The king was thought to share the divinity of the gods. It was believed that at his death, the king lost his human form and became a god, equal to the other gods. The king's burial place contained a temple at which he was worshiped as a god and where daily offerings of food and drink were made to him.[15]

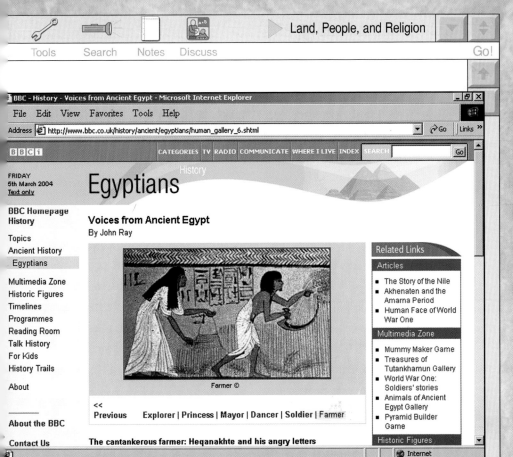

FRIDAY
5th March 2004
Text only

BBC Homepage
History

Topics
Ancient History
 Egyptians

Multimedia Zone
Historic Figures
Timelines
Programmes
Reading Room
Talk History
For Kids
History Trails

About

_____
About the BBC

Contact Us

Egyptians
History

Voices from Ancient Egypt
By John Ray

Farmer ©

<<
Previous   Explorer | Princess | Mayor | Dancer | Soldier | Farmer

The cantankerous farmer: Heqanakhte and his angry letters

Related Links

Articles
- The Story of the Nile
- Akhenaten and the Amarna Period
- Human Face of World War One

Multimedia Zone
- Mummy Maker Game
- Treasures of Tutankhamun Gallery
- World War One: Soldiers' stories
- Animals of Ancient Egypt Gallery
- Pyramid Builder Game

Historic Figures

Internet

The fertile Nile River valley and warm climate provided ancient Egyptians with excellent conditions for farming. Popular crops included barley, flax, grapes, lentils, onions, and wheat.

Despite changes in dynasties and rulers, including rule by foreigners, the basic forms of religious beliefs and ceremonies of the ancient Egyptians did not change much until the coming of Christianity under the Roman Empire. However, Amenhotep IV (1378–1352 B.C.) attempted to introduce a revolutionary change in Egypt's religion and culture. He changed his name from Amenhotep IV to Akhenaton, meaning "He Who Is of Service to Aton." Akhenaton attempted to make Aton, the sun god, the supreme god of Egypt. Worship of the

sun as the source of creation and all life was not new in Egypt, but Akhenaton's emphasis on the sole worship of Aton was.

Akhenaton closed many of the temples devoted to other gods and confiscated their property. The efforts to change the Egyptians' religious beliefs ended with Akhenaton's death. His successor, Tutankhamen, restored worship of the old gods and their temples. Tutankhamen described Akhenaton's rule as a mistake that left Egypt in a wretched condition.[16]

Akhenaton's monuments and temples were destroyed and his name deleted from the official king lists.[17] Worship of the old gods was revived, and the capital city built at Akhenaton named "Akhetaton" (modern-day Tel el Amarna) fell into ruin.

Existence After Death

The ancient Egyptians believed in an afterlife, so preservation of the deceased body was considered essential for the continued existence of Ka, an individual's lifeforce. To preserve the body, the internal organs were removed and stored in special urns, known as canopic jars, and the body was treated with certain herbs. After drying, the body was wrapped in layers of cloth, often fine linen, into which jewels and magic inscriptions were placed. Magic spells related to death and resurrection were repeated over the dead body. Such preserved bodies are popularly called mummies.

Osiris, Isis, Horus, and Set

Four of the many gods worshipped by ancient Egyptians were Osiris, the god of the underworld and Egypt's first king; his sister and wife, Isis, the mother goddess; their

Done   🌐 Internet

▲ *Akhenaton is best known in ancient Egyptian history for trying to change Egyptian worship from one of multiple gods to the worship of a single god. Although no one knows the pharaoh's reasons for this movement, Egyptian society returned to polytheism shortly after Akhenaton's death in 1352 B.C.*

son, Horus, god of the sky; and their brother, Set, god of wind and storms.

Many ancient Egyptians believed that Set, who was jealous of his brother Osiris, murdered him, cut up the body, and buried its parts in areas all over Egypt. Isis, after a long and difficult search, found the different parts of the body, reassembled them, and by magic restored Osiris to life. Horus, the son of Osiris and Isis, battled Set until Set recognized Horus as the king of mankind. The sun disk

became the symbol for Horus and was placed on the doors of all the temples in Egypt.

The story of Osiris, Isis, Horus, and Set, with its themes of resurrection after death and the struggle of good against evil, was a strong element of Egyptian culture and religion throughout the history of ancient Egypt.

▶ Pyramid and Coffin Texts

Scenes from the king's life and hieroglyphic texts of rites and prayers—intended to transform the king at his death to a god—decorated the king's tomb. These texts, known as the Pyramid Texts, are first found in the pyramid of King Unas (2375–2345 B.C.). The texts include the story of Osiris and identify the king with Osiris. Equally important, the Pyramid Texts included formulas for the priests to recite to assist the dead in their travels to the afterlife.

Coffin Texts consist of inscriptions written inside coffins. These include magic formulas given for the dead to gather (in the afterlife) with family and friends.

ARTS AND CULTURAL CONTRIBUTIONS

The great pyramids, colossal statues, and huge temple complexes, particularly at Karnak and Luxor, are perhaps the most striking examples of Egyptian art. Equally as important as these monuments are Egyptian painting, sculpture, and the murals and reliefs that decorate the walls of the temples and tombs themselves. Beyond all of these, skilled goldsmiths left a treasure trove of jewels within the pyramids and temples.

Along with the beautiful designs, paintings, and sculptures that decorate Egypt's monuments, there are inscriptions. These inscriptions often describe events, memorialize a pharaoh's reign, or simply name the person depicted. They have given historians valuable bits of information about the ancient Egyptian peoples.

▶ Pyramids

Based on the Egyptians' belief in life after death, pyramids were built as tombs for the kings and queens. Surrounding the pyramids were large complexes of temples and other buildings for priests and workers to carry out the daily services required for the king's existence in the afterlife.

There are many theories as to how the pyramids were built, including the use of ramps to allow the stones to be moved along as the pyramid rose, and pulleys and lifts to raise the massive blocks of stone. However, no solid evidence exists to show just how they were built.

The building of the pyramids is evidence of the great power of the Egyptian king and the wealth and prosperity of Egypt in the Old Kingdom. Vast amounts of resources, manpower, and the skill to organize them were required to build these massive structures.[1]

The Step Pyramid

The first of the great pyramids is known as the Step Pyramid. It is believed to be the world's first complete stone building. The Step Pyramid is made of six gigantic platforms, placed one above the other, like a series of steps. It rises 204 feet above the ground.

Imhotep built the Step Pyramid for King Djoser, the second king of the Third dynasty of the Old Kingdom. Imhotep, an official of the king, was not only a builder, but also a high priest, a scribe, and a man of great medical skill. In fact, he was later treated as a god and identified with the Greek god of healing.[2]

First True Pyramid and the Bent Pyramid

In 2613 B.C., Sneferu became king of Egypt and built as his tomb the first true pyramid. A true pyramid is a stone structure with a square base whose four sides are equal triangles that rise smoothly, inclining to a point above ground. Sneferu also built another pyramid, this one a bent pyramid whose sides abruptly change incline halfway up the pyramid.[3]

The Great Pyramid

The largest of the pyramids, the Great Pyramid, is the biggest stone building ever built. King Khufu, also known by the Greek name Cheops (2583–2560 B.C.), built the Great Pyramid. It contained nearly 6 million tons of

Egypt is known for its pyramids, including the Step Pyramid shown here. Completed circa 2630 B.C., it is thought to be the world's first building made of stone rather than mud brick.

stone and rose about 480 feet above the ground when it was built.[4]

Paintings and Reliefs

Egyptian paintings and reliefs in the tombs were not intended for the public. They were to assist the dead in the afterlife. The painting of hunts, banquets, and family gatherings would help the dead repeat those events in the afterlife.[5] Even though these events were painted according to a rigid, stylized formula, they show the daily life of the ancient Egyptians in realistic detail.

Paintings and reliefs did not represent the insight of a single artist but were the result of many craftsmen operating under a highly organized system of rules and

▲ Hunting in ancient Egypt was more than just a means of providing food. It was also a demonstration of the hunter's courage and his dominance over animals.

regulations. The style for depicting humans in Egyptian art developed as early as the Old Kingdom and continued in its basic form for about fifteen hundred years.[6]

▷ Akhenaton's Contribution to Art

King Akhenaton attempted to make Egyptian painting depict the human form in more natural and significantly less formal poses. Akhenaton with his wife, Queen Nefertiti, and their children are often shown in affectionate, informal family scenes. Instead of being painted as a robust hero, the king is shown as potbellied, with skinny arms and legs.[7] Following Akhenaton's death, this realism in art was largely abandoned.

▷ Jewelry Fashioned From Gold

The jewels fashioned by goldsmiths for both men and women are among the most beautiful and original ancient Egyptian artifacts. Magnificent masks of gold were placed over the face of the king's mummy. Jewels in the form of wide collars, bracelets, necklaces, earrings, rings, and anklets have been recovered from the tombs. The jewels are mostly made of gold, but some are silver, which was much scarcer in Egypt, and others are a mixture of gold and silver called electrum. Gems including carnelian, amethyst, lapis lazuli, turquoise, and jasper were often inlaid, or set into, the gold work.[8]

▷ Calendar

The calendar year, based on the daily appearance of the sun, was a major contribution to civilization from the Old Kingdom. The Egyptians divided the calendar year into twelve months of thirty days each. At the end of each year, five days were added. Each day was divided into twenty-four hours.[9] Today, a modified version of this calendar year is used throughout the world.

▷ Egyptian Hieroglyphs

Simply described, hieroglyphs are a form of picture writing. A picture of a duck can mean "duck," but it could also mean "son." To make clear the meaning of the hieroglyph, other pictures or signs were added. For example, if the picture was meant to depict a duck, a hieroglyph for bird was added to the duck hieroglyph.[10]

A more common form of writing for everyday use, known as hieratic, evolved in the Old Kingdom.[11] Hieratic writing consisted of cursive hieroglyphs. These

Back   Forward   Stop   Review   Home   Explore   Favorites   History

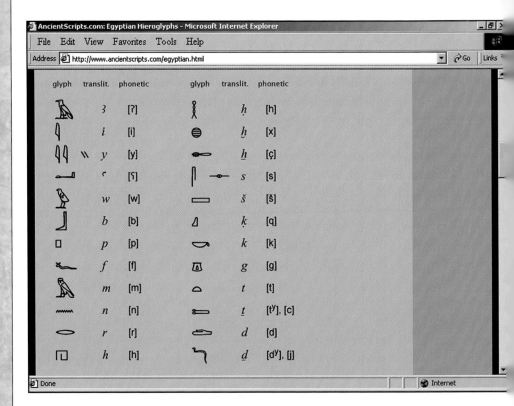

AncientScripts.com: Egyptian Hieroglyphs - Microsoft Internet Explorer

File   Edit   View   Favorites   Tools   Help

Address http://www.ancientscripts.com/egyptian.html

glyph	translit.	phonetic	glyph	translit.	phonetic
	ꜣ	[ʔ]		ḥ	[h]
	i	[i]		ḫ	[x]
	y	[y]		ẖ	[ç]
	ꜥ	[ʕ]		s	[s]
	w	[w]		š	[š]
	b	[b]		ḳ	[q]
	p	[p]		k	[k]
	f	[f]		g	[g]
	m	[m]		t	[t]
	n	[n]		ṯ	[tʸ], [c]
	r	[r]		d	[d]
	h	[h]		ḏ	[dʸ], [j]

Done   Internet

▲ *Ancient Egypt's hieroglyphs were used from approximately 3100 B.C. to A.D. 400, making them one of the world's oldest writing systems.*

abbreviated pictures or groups of strokes and dots sometimes looked very different from the original hieroglyphs. By the seventh century B.C., a third form of writing came into everyday use. It was a shortened version of hieratic known as demotic.

Since all forms of Egyptian writing omitted the use of signs to designate vowels, scholars have been unable to determine with certainty what the written language of the ancient Egyptians sounded like when spoken.[12]

Chapter 4 ▶

FAMILY LIFE AND EDUCATION

Men, women, and children of ancient Egypt lived in close-knit families. Paintings and other artwork depict husbands and wives with their children demonstrating affection for each other and in various family scenes. Most men had one wife, although kings and nobles sometimes had more than one wife.[1]

Marriage contracts provided for the wife's rights, particularly with regard to her property. Women had the right to dispose of their own property. Divorce by either the wife or husband was permitted. In the event of divorce, the wife's property was returned to her, and fathers were made to support their children.[2]

Egyptians valued order and balance in the universe and everyday life. In their temples and homes, they made daily offerings of food and drink to their gods to achieve that order.[3]

▶ Education

Children remained at home with their mothers until age four. Then, fathers began to educate their sons, and mothers began to teach their daughters. Farmers' children received little or no formal education. The boys learned the farming skills and crafts of their fathers; the girls learned the domestic skills of their mothers, particularly weaving. Above all, children in ancient Egypt were taught to honor their mothers.[4]

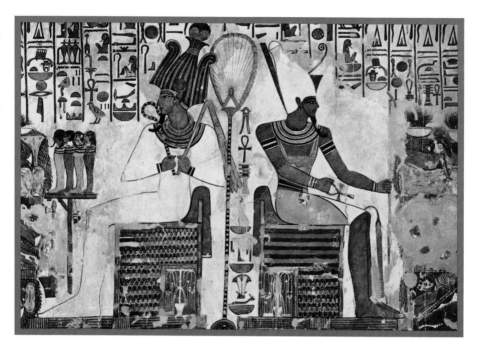

▲ *The east wall of Queen Nefertari's tomb features an image of offerings made to Osiris, the ruler of the dead, and Atum, the most powerful god. Nefertari was the wife of Ramses II.*

Most formal education was limited to boys of the wealthier classes. Most of these boys attended boarding schools, where they remained until age sixteen. Those boys who were intended for the priesthood or government service then went on to further study at temples or in government agencies.[5]

Reading and writing were basic in the schools administered by the government and the temples. Students learned by memorizing texts and then recording what they had memorized. Some students learned how to write letters and prepare documents by copying examples of these.[6] Studies also included ethics, a system of moral values, mathematics, athletics, and manners.[7]

Balls, models of crocodiles with movable jaws, and dolls (some of whose parts were moved by string) were among the typical toys of Egyptian children.[8] Ball games played by both children and adults were popular as were other outdoor activities.

Shelter

Houses in ancient Egypt ranged from the simple one-room mud hut of the poorest farmer to the more elaborate brick or stone home of the wealthy to the great palace complex of the king.

Houses generally were made of mud from the Nile baked into bricks or simply dried in the sun. A house might be a single room or a series of rooms built around one or more courtyards. The windows were covered with

▲ Like their ancestors, many Egyptians still build their homes using bricks made of mud.

mats woven from papyrus reeds. Most houses had a flat roof on which the family slept at night.[9]

Food

Bread was the staple food of the ancient Egyptians. It was made from wheat or barley flour and was ground in mortars with pestles or between two stones.[10] Geese and ducks grilled on a spit or roasted over a low hearth formed an important part of the Egyptian diet for wealthier families. The ancient Egyptians also ate fish, but in some districts, it was forbidden because the fish was considered holy or taboo. Beef, lamb, and goat were also part of the diet for the wealthy. Vegetables and herbs eaten by ancient Egyptians included onions, lentils, lettuces, garlic, and cucumbers. Fruits such as figs, dates, and grapes were grown throughout Egypt, and honey was used as a sweetener.

Clothing

For most of the people in the working classes of ancient Egypt, clothing was very simple. Men wore linen loincloths or kilts whose lengths could vary. They might wear shirts but usually did not. Women wore straight sleeveless linen dresses that could have one or two shoulder straps. These linen clothes were woven by women who used the fibers of the flax plant to make cloth.

Kings, priests, and other members of the elite class wore more elaborate clothing and had many different costumes for different ceremonies. The way their hair looked was also very important to the ancient Egyptians, not only for its appearance but also for what it meant in terms of social status. They used henna to dye graying hair and also wore wigs to hide baldness.

GOVERNMENT

Despite the changes in dynasties over three thousand years, the original system of government designed by the rulers of the Old Kingdom remained basically unchanged throughout the history of ancient Egypt.[1] The government was so stable and central to Egyptian civilization that it was able to survive internal rebellion from within its borders and attempted takeovers by foreign rulers.

▶ The Pharaoh

In ancient Egypt, the king was absolute ruler, high priest, and military commander in chief. He is frequently shown in battle and always victorious, even though some kings died in battle.[2]

His words when spoken, as written and interpreted by the king's officials, were the only body of law in ancient Egypt.[3] No other codes of law independent of the pharaoh are known to have existed. All officials governed in the king's name and only by his authority.

As high priest, the king was believed to be the only human who could communicate directly with the gods, and therefore was the only one suited to perform certain rites and ceremonies.

Throughout the history of ancient Egypt, there were challenges to the king's authority, especially at times when the king's power was reduced and the central government was weakened or deteriorated completely.

▷ Chief Administrator

The king's chief minister, the tjaty or vizier, handled the day-to-day workings of government in ancient Egypt. His power extended over a population estimated at 2 million in the Old Kingdom and 3 million in the New Kingdom.[4]

Under the Old Kingdom, Pepi II appointed a separate minister for Upper and Lower Egypt. As time went on, a large bureaucracy formed that was mostly composed of scribes, men trained in Egyptian forms of writing. Officials were appointed to specialized departments such as the treasury, which collected taxes, and agriculture, which dealt with cultivating the land and harvesting crops.

During periods when the king's authority was not challenged, the government's administrators, acting

▲ Ramses II, also known as Ramses the Great, is one of Egypt's most famous pharaohs. His sixty-seven-year reign was a time of great prosperity. Pictured is the Great Temple of Ramses II, located in Nubia.

through the absolute power of the king, were able to organize all of Egypt's resources for the king's enormous construction projects. This was particularly true during the Old Kingdom. Thousands of workers came from all over Egypt to work on the pyramids, tombs, temples, and monuments.[5] This was also likely to happen during periods when farming was not possible, such as during the flooding of the Nile. In addition to the materials needed for the projects, enormous resources of food, clothing, and other materials were required for the workers and their families.

Nomes, Nomarchs, and Priests

Nomarchs, appointed by the king of Egypt, administered the districts called nomes into which Egypt was divided. Over the years, the office of nomarch became an inherited office. At times, the nomarchs became powerful enough to challenge the king and central government.[6]

The priests of Egypt, under the authority of the king, also helped oversee the government. They supervised the great temple estates located throughout Egypt, each with large numbers of workers, and directed the storage and distribution of the harvests.

Money and Taxes

Except for the use of gold, some silver, and other metals such as copper and bronze, whose value was determined by weight, there was no money in ancient Egypt.[7] Payment for work on the huge building projects was in the form of rations and goods distributed by the government. Buying and selling between ordinary individuals and traders was mainly by barter. A jar of fat and lumps of metal might be exchanged for an ox.[8]

HISTORY AND CONQUEST

The kings of the first two dynasties of the Old Kingdom established the basic form of central government rule by an absolute king that lasted throughout the history of ancient Egypt. The term "pharaoh," meaning "king," came into use in the late New Kingdom. Before that, it referred to the "great house" of the king.[1]

Menes, the first king of Egypt, is credited with unifying Upper and Lower Egypt. Menes may be legendary, but it is clear that unification came about through domination of Lower Egypt by Upper Egypt.[2] Upon unification, Memphis became the capital city for all of Egypt. Memphis remained one of the capital cities throughout the rest of ancient Egypt's history.

King Merenre of the Sixth dynasty sent expeditions into Syria and Palestine. He also expanded Egypt's rule into northern Nubia to the south of the Third Cataract.[3] Otherwise the Old Kingdom remained mostly at peace.

The reign of Pepi II, the last king of the Old Kingdom, lasted from fifty to seventy years. The growth of the number of governors, or nomarchs, during this period was significant.[4]

▶ End of the Old Kingdom

By about 2200 B.C., toward the end of the Old Kingdom, the office of nomarch had become an inherited office, from father to son. This development further weakened the power of the king and central government. Nomarchs divided Egypt between rulers from the city of Thebes and the city of Herakleopolis. Finally, about 1980 B.C., Nebhepetre Mentuhotep II, a king from Thebes, defeated the Herakleopolitan king and Egypt was reunited. A new dynasty established by Amenemhet I, a former minister of Mentuhotep II, began the Middle Kingdom.[5]

▷ Middle Kingdom

The unity and prosperity of Egypt was established again under the Middle Kingdom. Amenemhet II (1818–1772 B.C.) appointed two ministers—one for Upper Egypt, the other for Lower Egypt—to administer the government.

▲ The Valley of the Kings contains sixty-two tombs dating from the New Kingdom. It is believed that its location on the West Bank of the Nile River behind the Thebian Hills was chosen because the area is small, easily guarded, and surrounded by steep cliffs.

The kings who reigned in the Middle Kingdom launched expeditions into Libya, Syria, Palestine, and Nubia.[6] Except for parts of northern Nubia, Egypt did not annex or incorporate foreign territory. Instead, it left troops in the conquered areas to secure Egypt's borders against invaders. In addition, these garrisons protected trade routes and access to resources in the areas.

▶ Second Intermediate Period: The Hyksos

A small number of Asiatic tribes known as the Hyksos brought about the end of the Middle Kingdom. The Hyksos, who had settled in the Delta, gradually gained control of Lower Egypt and became its rulers, possibly with the help of Nubia. These rulers belong to the Fifteenth dynasty.[7]

The Hyksos did not impose their culture or form of government on Egypt. Instead, as did later conquerors of Egypt, they adopted the forms and practices of the Egyptian kings, including their religion and royal titles. The most important contribution the Hyksos made to

The Temple of Ramses II at Luxor.

Egypt was to increase Egypt's military might. The Hyksos introduced the harnessed horse, a two-wheel chariot, body armor, and new weapons.[8]

For a time, an Egyptian king from Thebes continued to rule Lower Egypt, but eventually even the Theban ruler recognized the rule of the Hyksos.[9]

New Kingdom

Kamose, an Egyptian king in Thebes, went to war with the Hyksos, greatly reducing the Hyksos king's power. However, it was his brother Ahmose (1539–1514 B.C.) who finally defeated and expelled the Hyksos and unified Egypt. Ahmose's son, Thutmose I, was considered the founder of the Eighteenth dynasty under which the New Kingdom began.[10]

Thutmose I returned the capital of Egypt to Memphis, and Thebes became the center of the worship of Amun with the great temple at Karnak. A great new burial ground of royal tombs known as the Valley of the Kings was begun with the burial there of Thutmose II.[11]

Egypt became an imperial power during the New Kingdom. Thutmose III, who ascended to the throne after the death of his stepmother, Hatshepsut, became Egypt's greatest military ruler. He extended Egypt's southern border to the Fourth Cataract in Nubia and conquered Gaza, Palestine, and Syria. Peace between Egypt and the Mitanni Empire (Syria) was finally established when both were threatened by a new power, the Hittites.

Hittites

By 1328 B.C., the Hittites, originally from Anatolia (now Turkey), had conquered most of Syria.[12] The Hittite king had become so powerful that Tutankhamen's widow

asked to marry one of his sons. That son would have become king of Egypt if he had not been murdered on his arrival.

About 1275 or 1274 B.C., Ramses II of the Nineteenth dynasty met the Hittites in a great battle at Kadesh. The temple walls of Ramses II boast of a great victory, but in reality there was no decisive victory. As a result, Egypt and the Hittites remained independent of each other. In 1269 B.C., Egypt, threatened in the west by Libyan forces and the Hittites and in the east by the Assyrians, entered into a peace treaty with the Hittites. Later, marriages between the two kings' families reinforced the treaty.[13]

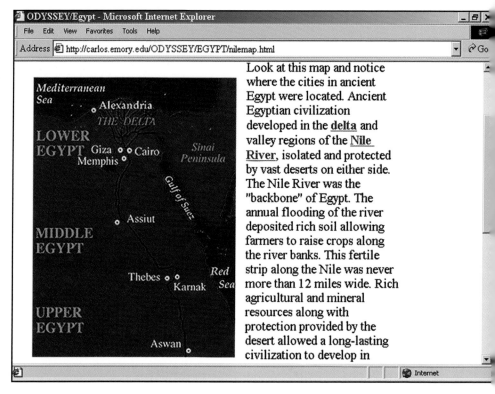

ODYSSEY/Egypt - Microsoft Internet Explorer

File   Edit   View   Favorites   Tools   Help

Address http://carlos.emory.edu/ODYSSEY/EGYPT/nilemap.html   Go

Look at this map and notice where the cities in ancient Egypt were located. Ancient Egyptian civilization developed in the delta and valley regions of the Nile River, isolated and protected by vast deserts on either side. The Nile River was the "backbone" of Egypt. The annual flooding of the river deposited rich soil allowing farmers to raise crops along the river banks. This fertile strip along the Nile was never more than 12 miles wide. Rich agricultural and mineral resources along with protection provided by the desert allowed a long-lasting civilization to develop in

Mediterranean Sea
Alexandria
THE DELTA
LOWER EGYPT   Giza   Cairo
Memphis
Sinai Peninsula
Gulf of Suez
Assiut
MIDDLE EGYPT
Thebes   Red
Karnak   Sea
UPPER EGYPT
Aswan

Internet

This map shows the location of the important cities of ancient Egypt that developed along the Nile.

Ramses II was succeeded by a series of kings who also were named Ramses. These kings and their governments became progressively weaker. Upon the death of Ramses XI, rule of Egypt was divided between rulers in Tanis, a city on a branch of the Nile, and the Amun priesthood in Thebes.[14]

The Third Intermediate Period

The Third Intermediate Period lasted more than four hundred years and was a time of divided rule in Egypt. Libyans, Nubians, and Assyrians succeeded each other in ruling all or parts of Egypt.[15]

Foreign rule produced a notable change in the king's role in religion. In this period, the priests in Thebes increasingly took over the role of the pharaoh in temple ceremonies, and women became prominent in certain sectors of religion. The temple services became more focused on the daughter of the king or high priest as the "god's wife."[16] For the most part, however, the foreign rulers adopted the titles and ceremonies of the pharaoh in Egypt, and life among the ordinary Egyptians continued as it had for centuries.

Late Period

By 656 B.C., Egyptian Prince Psamtek (664–610 B.C.) from the city of Sais in the Delta had ended Assyrian domination and reunited Egypt.[17] In the Late Period, there appears to have been extensive trading with the Greek city-states, and the Egyptians again advanced to the Euphrates River for a brief time. Wars were conducted with Nubia, Libya, and a new power, the Chaldaeans, in the east. However, the greatest threat to Egypt appeared in the form of the new and expanding Persian Empire.

Persian Conquerors

Egypt's independence ended in 525 B.C., with its conquest by Cambyses, king of Persia and son of Cyrus the Great, creator of the Persian Empire. Egypt was made a province of the Persian Empire.

Cambyses took the role and title of pharaoh, kept the Egyptian form of government in place, and honored the Egyptians' gods. His successor, Darius I, continued the practice, restoring temples and monuments and increasing the revenue of the temples.[18]

In 404 B.C., Amyrtaios, an Egyptian, declared himself king and rebelled against Persia. Under Amyrtaios, the

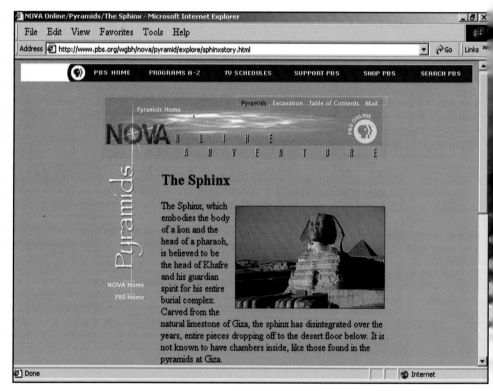

Egypt's Great Sphinx contains a human head atop a lion's body. This statue, built circa 2530 B.C., is badly eroded due to the material used in its construction, soft limestone.

Egyptians maintained their independence from 404 B.C. to 343 B.C., when the Persian king Artaxerxes III overcame them. However, Persia's rule of Egypt was then threatened by a new power, the Greeks, led by Alexander the Great, king of Macedonia.

▶ Alexander the Great

In 332 B.C., Alexander the Great, after conquering the Persian Empire, invaded and conquered Egypt. There was no great battle; the Egyptians greeted Alexander as a liberator. The priests at Thebes recognized Alexander as the new ruler of Egypt and named him pharaoh, with the double crown of Upper and Lower Egypt. Alexander accepted with sincere belief in the traditions and religious role of the pharaoh, making sacrifices to the Egyptian gods and restoring the temples at Karnak and Luxor.[19]

Alexander's greatest achievement in Egypt was the founding of a new capital city, Alexandria, on the Mediterranean Sea. Alexandria would become one of the richest and most important cities of the ancient world.

In 323 B.C., Alexander died, and his generals then carved up his empire. One of them, Ptolemy I, took Egypt as his kingdom. Ptolemy's successors ruled Egypt until the suicide of Cleopatra in 30 B.C., when Egypt became the personal property of the Roman emperor.[20]

Chapter 1. Hatshepsut—King of Egypt

1. Joyce Tyldesley, *Hatchepsut, The Female Pharaoh* (New York: Penquin Books USA, Inc., 1996), p. 99.

2. Gay Robins, *Women In Ancient Egypt* (Cambridge, Mass.: Harvard University Press, 1993), p. 51.

3. Barbara Watterson, *Women in Ancient Egypt* (Gloucestershire, Great Britain: Sutton Publishing Limited, 1991), p. 140.

4. Tyldesley, p. 143.

5. Ibid., pp. 145–146.

6. Ian Shaw, *The Oxford History of Ancient Egypt* (New York: Oxford University Press, Inc., 2000), p. 243.

7. Ibid., p. 243.

Chapter 2. Land, People, and Religion

1. Amélie Kuhrt, *The Ancient Near East, c.3000–330 B.C.* (New York: Routledge, 1995), p. 118.

2. Chester G. Starr, *A History of the Ancient World* (New York: Oxford University Press, 1971), p. 55.

3. Kuhrt, p. 124.

4. Starr, p. 53.

5. Kuhrt, p. 120.

6. Barry J. Kemp, *Ancient Egypt, Anatomy of a Civilization* (New York: Routledge, 1991), p. 10.

7. Adolf Erman, *Life in Ancient Egypt* (New York: Dover Publications, Inc., 1971), p. 448.

8. Ibid., p. 447.

9. Pierre Montet, *Eternal Egypt* (New York: The New American Library of World Literature, Inc.. 1964), p. 21.

10. Ibid., pp. 96–97.

11. David P. Silverman, ed., *Ancient Egypt* (New York: Oxford University Press, 1997), p. 86.

12. Ibid., p. 162.

13. Erman, p. 307.

14. Ibid., p. 272.

15. Esmond Wright, ed., *History of the World* (Middlesex, Great Britain: Newnes Books, a division of The Hamlyn Publishing Group Limited, 1985), p. 57.

16. Nicholas Grimal, translated by Ian Shaw, *A History of Ancient Egypt* (Oxford, Great Britain: Blackwell Publishers, 1992), p. 241.

17. Silverman, p. 152.

Chapter 3. Arts and Cultural Contributions

1. Claudio Barocas, *Egypt* (New York: Grosset & Dunlap, 1972), p. 24.

2. Sir Alan Gardiner, *The Egyptians, An Introduction* (London: The Folio Society—Oxford University Press, 1961), p. 69.

3. Barocas, p. 27.

4. Chester G. Starr, *A History of the Ancient World* (New York: Oxford University Press, 1971), p. 58.

5. Sir J. Gardner Wilkinson, *The Ancient Egyptians, Their Life and Gods, Vol. I* (London: Studio Editions, Ltd., 1990), pp. 86–87.

6. Irmgard Woldering, *The Art of Egypt, The Time of the Pharoahs* (New York: Greystone Press, 1965), p. 95.

7. Ibid., p. 170.

8. Barbara Watterson, *Women in Ancient Egypt* (Gloucestershire, Great Britain: Sutton Publishing Limited, 1991), pp. 106–107.

9. Starr, p. 62.

10. Nicholas Grimal, translated by Ian Shaw, *A History of Ancient Egypt* (Oxford, Great Britain: Blackwell Publishers, 1992), p. 33.

11. Adolf Erman, *Life in Ancient Egypt* (New York: Dover Publications, Inc., 1971), p. 339.

12. Jacquetta Hawkes, *The First Great Civilizations: Life in Mesopotamia, the Indus Valley, and Egypt* (New York: Alfred A. Knopf, 1977), p. 438.

Chapter 4. Family Life and Education

1. Adolf Erman, *Life in Ancient Egypt* (New York: Dover Publications, Inc., 1971), p. 151.

2. Esmond Wright, ed., *History of the World* (Middlesex, Great Britain: Newnes Books, a division of The Hamlyn Publishing Group Limited, 1985), p. 87.

3. David P. Silverman, ed., *Ancient Egypt* (New York: Oxford University Press, 1997), p. 148.

4. Erman, p. 155.

5. Barbara Watterson, *Women in Ancient Egypt* (Gloucestershire, Great Britain: Sutton Publishing Limited, 1991), p. 124.

6. Wright, p. 88.

7. Erman, p. 165.

8. Sir J. Gardner Wilkinson, *The Ancient Egyptians, Their Life and Gods, Vol. I* (London: Studio Editions, Ltd., 1990), pp. 196–197.

9. Ibid., p. 7.

10. Erman, p. 189.

Chapter 5. Government

1. Nicholas Grimal, translated by Ian Shaw, *A History of Ancient Egypt* (Oxford, Great Britain: Blackwell Publishers, 1992), p. 93.

2. David P. Silverman, ed., *Ancient Egypt* (New York: Oxford University Press, 1977), pp. 108–109.

3. Grimal, p. 58.

4. Esmond Wright, ed., *History of the World* (Middlesex, Great Britain: Newnes Books, a division of The Hamlyn Publishing Group Limited, 1985), p. 94.

5. Silverman, p. 67.

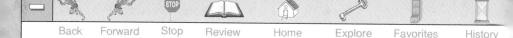

6. Ibid., p. 27.

7. Barry J. Kemp, *Ancient Egypt, Anatomy of a Civilization* (New York: Routledge, 1991), p. 117.

8. Ibid., p. 248.

Chapter 6. History and Conquest

1. David P. Silverman, ed., *Ancient Egypt* (New York: Oxford University Press, 1997), p. 109.

2. Nicholas Grimal, translated by Ian Shaw, *A History of Ancient Egypt* (Oxford, Great Britain: Blackwell Publishers, 1992), p. 48.

3. Ibid., p. 87.

4. Silverman, p. 26.

5. Ibid., p. 27.

6. Grimal, p. 155.

7. Ibid., pp. 185–186.

8. Joyce Tyldesley, *Hatchepsut, The Female Pharaoh* (New York: Penguin Books USA, Inc., 1996), p. 21.

9. Silverman, p. 31.

10. Grimal, pp. 192–193.

11. Kuhrt, p. 191.

12. O.R. Gurney, *The Hittites* (London: The Folio Society—Penguin Books Inc., 1990), p. 28.

13. Kuhrt, p. 207.

14. Ibid., p. 210.

15. Ibid., p. 623.

16. Ian Shaw, *The Oxford History of Ancient Egypt* (New York: Oxford University Press Inc., 2000), pp. 359–360.

17. Ibid., p. 371.

18. Jacquetta Hawkes, *The First Great Civilizations: Life in Mesopotamia, the Indus Valley, and Egypt* (New York: Alfred A. Knopf, 1977), p. 321.

19. Peter Green, *Alexander of Macedon 356–323 B.C.* (Berkeley and Los Angeles: University of California Press, 1991), pp. 269–270.

20. Grimal, pp. 2–3.

Further Reading

Ardagh, Philip. *Ancient Egypt.* Columbus, Ohio: McGraw-Hill Children's Publishing, 2000.

Baines, John, and Jaromir Malek. *Cultural Atlas of Ancient Egypt.* New York: Facts on File, 2000.

Caselli, Giovanni. *In Search of Tutankhamen: The Discovery of a King's Tomb.* Columbus, Ohio: McGraw-Hill Children's Publishing, 2001.

Greenblatt, Miriam. *Hatshepsut and Ancient Egypt.* New York: Benchmark Books, 1999.

Kallen, Stuart A. *Pyramids.* Farmington Hills, Mich.: Gale Group, 2002.

Kaplan, Leslie C. *Art and Religion in Ancient Egypt.* New York: PowerKids Press, 2004.

Meltzer, Milton. *In the Days of the Pharaohs: A Look at Ancient Egypt.* New York: Franklin Watts, 2001.

Millard, Anne. *The World of the Pharaoh.* Columbus, Ohio: McGraw-Hill Children's Publishing, 2001.

Morris, Neil. *Ancient Egypt.* Columbus, Ohio: McGraw-Hill Children's Publishing, 2000.

Nardo, Don. *Ancient Egypt.* San Diego: Lucent Books, 2003.

———. *Egyptian Mythology.* Berkeley Heights, N.J.: Enslow Publishers, Inc., 2001.

Pemberton, Delia. *Egyptian Mummies: People From the Past.* San Diego: Harcourt, 2001.

Rumford, James. *Seeker of Knowledge: The Man Who Deciphered Egyptian Hieroglyphs.* Boston: Houghton Mifflin, 2000.

Sims, Lesley. A *Visitor's Guide to Ancient Egypt.* Tulsa: EDC Publishing, 2001.

Streissguth, Thomas. *Life in Ancient Egypt.* Farmington Hills, Mich.: Gale Group, 2000.

Index